Confessions of A Masochist

by Peter Cohen

Table of Contents

Confessions of A Masochist

I first noticed that I had the problem of enjoying punishment and beatings when I was ten years old. At that time, the other boys used to take turns beating me up. I loved it.

When I turned 13, I became strongly attracted to females and my masochism turned to fantasies about being beaten by females. For 49 years, I dreamed of being beaten up by nice women. This would only happen off and on when my mental health was not very good.

When I turned 15, I took up boxing at a psychiatrist's suggestion, the same psychiatrist that caused my schizophrenia. Muhammad Ali was a great inspiration to me. He punched just hard enough to win and come out of the ring without a scratch. He was also a great humanitarian. His secret was quantity and quality of training. He also had a great deal of ability, which I did not particularly have. This training and the practice and competition of boxing put my masochism into remission. I no longer had to identify with an aggressor and my unrealistic conscience was in remission.

However, when I was 18, I was railroaded into a Nazi-like death camp. This made the masochism much worse.

The cause of masochism was excessive conscience and a taboo against aggression and a denial of my own very aggressive nature. I would often identify with an aggressor or be punished to appease my conscience. This was even before my full-blown schizophrenia caused inappropriate violence and aggression. Toxic women and poor mental health would draw out the masochism more. Finally, when I was 34, I asked my girl friend to hit me hard. She said "no way." My Sz medication had stopped working then.

Now, I got my wife into a bad habit of hitting me, and I call and try to visit dominatrices. This occupies much of my thinking and time.

Often, I cannot get turned on unless a woman hits me. Even when I hit myself, it excites me.

I find being hit to be my strongest turn-on as opposed to being caned, over-humiliated, or pinched. Even when I hit myself, I get excited and fantasize women hitting me. It has become a real problem.

In some ways, I was taught that liking pain was a sign of manhood. However, this is illogical and intellectually I believe it to be untrue. When I understand it on an emotional level, I will begin to recover. Next, I will present some accounts of my experiences with dominatrices. Before that, I will discuss gender identity and coping with masochism.

Gender Identity

Gender is your physical appearance of being either male or female or whatever. Gender identity is a matter partly of what gender you want to be. Cross gender identity is a matter of wanting to be a gender other than your physical phenotype. When you feel you have manhood or womanhood I call it adequate gender identity. It is very important. When you do not feel you have achieved manhood or womanhood, I call it inferior gender identity. It is a very serious condition and is a cause of major problems and a part of many mental illnesses, including schizophrenia, as I have experienced. It can cause masochism, self-harm, putting people down, and even violence and murder. That is why I always advocate treating each other, men and women with dignity and respect. A statement against one's manhood after the age of thirteen or even younger is inhuman. The same goes for females.

Manhood or womanhood is something you feel you have achieved as a man or woman you admire. It may include striving for certain qualities you want to achieve, in younger people. However, it should never be something you cannot achieve and feel you do not have. It only has a small amount to do with age. Anyone who feels that he is genetically inferior as my family would like to believe has a major problem as I described earlier. I even remember someone hating me enough to try to murder me because of this.

Suggestions for Coping with Masochism

- Accept the masochism if it does not hurt anybody. If you need to believe that it is a sign of manhood or womanhood, that is OK as long as it does not hurt anybody.

- Review triggers for your masochism and avoid them.

- Maintain your best mental health possible and realize that masochism is bad and gently try to stop.

- Seek ways to build your self-esteem without masochism.

- Seek constructive outlets for your aggression.

- Seek alternatives to masochism.

Masochism is defined as deriving sexual pleasure out of being punished, beaten, having ill-health or bad luck. It is partly caused by inferiority feelings and has the biopsychosocial model as most mental illnesses do. It is also caused by holding in or denying feelings, some of which can be dangerous like certain types of aggression.

We must recognize that no person is better than another as some people have put me down for having schizophrenia, that we are all equal. Paranoid schizophrenia causes delusions of grandeur as does schizotypal personality disorder. We must fight against these tendencies.

A Heroine Named Heidi and The Adventures of Superwoman

More beautiful than a beauty queen.

More luscious than a love goddess.

Able to mesmerize strong men in a single glance. Look!

It's a Playboy Playmate!

It's a picture!

No, it's Superwoman. Superwoman, strange visitor from another planet who came to earth with the power and ability to excite men far beyond that of mortal women. Superwoman, who can change the course of mighty armies, bend a man like putty in her bare hands;

And who disguised as Heidi Gabriel, mild-mannered sports therapist for a great Metropolitan practice, fights a never-ending battle for truth, justice and the Canadian way.

Feats:

- She earned her black belt Tae Kwon Do.
- She became a fantastic professional boxer, even beating men.
- She taught bullies lessons.
- She helped many people heal.
- She established a risky sports therapy practice.
- She helped many people with her kindness and generosity.
- She uses her extreme beauty to help people and erase pain.
- She loved and accepted many people, some marginalized.
- She excelled at many sports.
- She became a social worker and helped save many children, sometimes putting herself in danger.
- She showed extreme tolerance for pain and fearlessness in many situations.
- She did the equivalent of looking down the muzzle of a loaded gun with an epileptic at the trigger.
- She defeated a man who could have turned into a monster.
- She excelled at academics, even being accepted at

university with a 3.5 grade point average, very high.

- She overcame a turbulent beginning and background and learned to help people.
- She overcame homelessness, even at the young age of 11.
- She became a great mother.
- She defeated the former men's city champion at boxing, who was 50 pounds weight advantage.
- She trained to exhaustion at long distance running, weight training and boxing.
- She survived on the street at a young age using her wits.
- She did above and beyond the call of duty in her job and showed a lot of generosity.
- She was a warm and generous friend.
- She took a leadership role in a competitive business.
- She confronts men in risky situations and overcomes fear with love.
- She forgives and forgets.
- She takes risks to help friends.
- She takes risks to help the poor, disadvantaged, and downtrodden.
- She has the courage to accept and display her sexuality.
- She handles her extreme beauty with grace and modesty.
- She cooks well.

- She is a good wrestler.
- She has excellent physical strength and can do chinups.
- She is not afraid to hit a man hard.
- She worked and paid taxes in spite of numerous problems.
- She keeps fit in spite of health problems.
- She cut down on smoking.
- She overcame many addictions.
- She maintains spirituality in spite of many problems.
- She maintains her femininity while excelling at typically "guy" things like boxing and wrestling.
- She shows great courage in helping people with her athletic prowess and intervenes in situations when someone needs help.
- She tells people off when she gets angry.
- She handles her alter-ego well and maintains her secret identity.
- She is open-minded and without prejudice.
- She is emotionally satisfying as well as physically satisfying.
- She holds her own when streetfighting with men.
- She follows the serenity prayer – God grant me the serenity to accept the things I cannot change, courage to change the things I can and the wisdom to know the difference.
- She appreciates the good in all people.

- She is an excellent lover.

- She maintains assertion.

- She maintains independence.

- She understands people's problems.

- She respects people's privacy and individual lives.

- She does an honest and fearless appraisal of her strengths and weaknesses and has a realistic opinion of herself.

- She accepts other people's strengths and weaknesses.

- She breaks down racial, cultural, sexual, and socio-economic barriers.

- She is a liberated feminist who still appreciates men.

- She respects the spirit of the law.

- She excels at both interpersonal and solitary pursuits.

- She respects her children and her family.

- She maintains a good sense of humour.

- She is more than beauty and uses her physical self for action and good as well as being generous in displaying her beauty.

- She is unspoiled.

- She graduated from the college of hard knocks with honours.

I first met Heidi as a patient of her sports therapy practice. I researched ads for people who did sports therapy and similar services and hers looked to be the best at a reasonable price. She looked good in her picture, but when I met her she looked much better than in the picture, one of the most beautiful women I have ever seen.

I called her and told her that I was a very bad man and wanted to get beaten up. She said, "You came to the right woman. I'm a really good boxer and very strong." I waited until I had a day off and saved 100 dollars for the therapy.

I called her incessantly the night before I saw her. She said, "What's up."

I told her that I was bothered by guilt.

She said, "Don't worry. I'll beat the crap out of you."

She asked, "Are you frightened?"

"A little," I said.

She said, "You should be. You're going to get your ass kicked!"

When I got to her place, I opened the door gingerly, expecting mercilessness and pain.

I asked, "Is the champ here?"

"I'm down here waiting for you," she said.

I carefully walked down the stairs and was stunned by what I saw. There was this beautiful woman with milk chocolate skin, interspersed with specks of caramel, her skin smooth and blemish-free. She was brazenly standing there, completely naked. Her feet were cute, leading to legs of statuesque femininity, like pylons, rounding into thighs that led to an hourglass figure of sensuous hips, a flat, fit belly, muscular shoulders, and muscular arms. She stood about five foot five and weighed about 125 pounds. Best of all, her breasts came full and round against her muscular chest, more like the goddess, Venus. They were plump and firm and she almost knocked me out by letting me look at her. Her black hair fell straight down to her shoulders and her lips were full and heavy. The look on her face was intense, denoting depth of character, which I later found out was true. Her nipples were budded, like dark plums, and pointed sumptuously. She must have descended from the heavens as I later found out her name, Gabriel implied, an archangel sent to heal me.

She said, "Take off your clothes and show me where you want the marks and bruises."

Excitedly, I undressed, down to only an erection. She playfully squeezed my nipples and whacked my buttocks. She put a ball in my mouth so I would not make noise, but I took it out soon as it was unnecessary. I told her that I liked to be punched in the face. She started giving me delightful slaps and punches in the face and body and began working me over with delicious slaps and punches. We paused to talk and hug and kiss often. I asked her for some left hooks and six-punch combinations to the face and body, which she obliged. I told her hesitantly that I loved her because I was very excited and fond of her. She started telling me about herself and it was a hair-raising story of abuse and her response with courage. I will present the story and share some emails. Incidentally, she was a fabulous boxer and martial artist. She puffed up and decorated my face professionally. She did it with kindness, gentleness, and love. My penis was leaking semen and came close to her vulva. She said she had an IUD put in. Not only did she never hurt me, but her therapy was to convert mental pain into something physical to cause healing. Mental pain is much worse than physical pain and she had tremendous compassion. She has the sweetest pair of fists in all of Toronto and uses them to help people. She also has the sweetest pair of knockers in Toronto and uses them to help people. She could have broken me like a matchstick or made me into a willing slave with her sexiness, but she chose to be merciful.

Heidi was born in Trinidad, the biological daughter of a whore and an unknown client.

Heidi's Early Days

Heidi was dropped off at a nursery with nuns in Toronto by her mother. Her mother used her father, a good Englishman, to get into Canada and dropped him once she was safely in Canada. She may also have caused his death soon after. She had no conscience and murdered someone and got away with it, hiding the bloody remains. She is one of the few people Heidi was afraid of, due to this apparent psychopathy.

Her mother said, "Aren't you lucky, Heidi. These nice ladies will take care of you."

Bullroar!

They threw her around like a rag doll. They let her go hungry and cry, without any warmth, comfort, or love. They would have intercourse with men right in front of her.

"Eat the nice milk from our bodies, Heidi. It's good for you" they said.

"I don't want to," Heidi protested.

"Eat it or we'll knock you flying," they said.

Heidi would eat the semen repeatedly and vomit or risk many beatings. Heidi was later adopted by a family of perverts who treated her much the same way. This can have serious consequences for a child's development. Heidi did not realize how bad they were until much later just like I did not realize how bad the doctor who caused my schizophrenia was until too late. She did not realize that the situation was traumatic just like I did not realize my situation was traumatic.

Heidi was eventually adopted by a good family, a deacon at a church and his wife. She remained loyal to all her siblings. I remember telling her about a romantic fictional story about a brother who raped his later to be movie star sister.

She said, "My brother did not have to rape me, he just had to ask me."

Getting back to the nunnery, as bad a Heidi's mother was, the nuns were worse. Heidi went from the frying pan into the fire. This would happen many other times in Heidi's life and she would trade a bad situation in for something worse.

Heidi would often read negative connotations into my tone and words and actions, when actually I meant no harm. This might have happened with others as well. After Heidi got more and more angry with me, due to my perceived conceit, which was actually delusions of grandeur caused by Sz, I lost contact with her for a few months.

Later, she called and said she was living with a nice guy named Jeff. I was delighted and said that I was happy for her. It turned out there was nothing to be happy about. He was a total monster. He made a lucrative living out of selling illegal drugs. He never gave her a penny and she was often hungry. He would open her mail, monitor her and would not let her eat unless she was fed by hand, a terrible indignity. He would hit her and kick her and call her a whore and many other obscenities. He even kicked her in her smashed leg, causing tremendous pain. He made her look after all his many needs but never cared when she was suffering. He only took and did not give.

The situation that she left was loneliness, homelessness, and not having a significant other. Often it is natural to want a solution to these problems and then use "sweet lemon" rationalization for the worse situation. When I tried to take Heidi away from this man at a cancer hospital, I could not find her and she would not answer my desperate calls to find out where she was. It was very frustrating.

Heidi's father, a friend and I tried to get her out of the situation with little success. This is part of the "battered woman syndrome." Heidi's father and friend were great and dedicated heroes. She eventually came out.

Even though I love my wife dearly, I love Heidi, too, and also want all of you to love such a good woman who deserves good treatment. Please ask God to love her in your prayers.

Heroine Heidi vs. The Former City Champion

In this corner, weighing 182 pounds the former city champion of Toronto, Pete The Bully (boos).

In this corner, weighing 133 pounds, former Miss Universe, Heidi The Heroine Gabriel, nicknamed "Sweet-fists" for her dazzling fighting style (yay, yay).

Pete, do you respect Heidi?

"I respect all fighters, go to the gym and work, especially her."

The Bully is so cocky, he allows the challenger not to wear gloves.

The referee is laying down the rules. "Let's have a good, clean fight. Keep your clothes on at all times. No spitting, hair-pulling, or hitting after the bell. Otherwise all's fair. Now hug and kiss and come out fighting."

The former champion comes out in his blue trunks and throws a vicious jab and straight right at the challenger. She leans away. The former champ follows a left-right with a left hook, which the challenger deftly ducks under and throws a tremendous left-right combination followed by her famous left hook. The former champ backs off and Heidi pours punches into his face and body. She is punching on balance and in combinations, the sign of a talented fighter.

The former champ hugs her and kisses her and she responds with a long hug and kiss. The referee breaks them up. He caught a glimpse of Heidi's figure! Now he is down and he is stunned. He struggles to his feet after an eight count, his blue shorts bulging. The challenger turns and then straightens up to show her full figure, followed by a six-punch combination.

The former champion is face down unconscious and the count is starting. The Bully is not getting up. Heroine Heidi is the new champion of both men and women! The crowd is ecstatic. They are shouting, Hei-di, Hei-di!

The doctor has been called and the referee has raised Heroine Heidi's hand in triumph. The former champ rolls over on his back and is conscious now. The heroine puts her foot on his belly in triumph.

The former champion gets up on his hands and knees shouting, "You're the greatest! You're the prettiest!" He crawls over to Heidi and is kissing her feet. He gets up and says,

"I love you, Heidi, you taught me a good lesson."

He hugs her and kisses her and they go to their dressing rooms.

Heidi vs. The Incredible Hulk

When I was sixteen and being treated for a bogus depression, I was accidentally bombarded by catecholamine chemicals from tricyclic antidepressants that altered my body chemistry. After that, when I would become angry or outraged, a startling metamorphosis would occur. I would turn into something like the 7 foot, 500 pound monster, The Hulk. I would become mindless and driven by rage. This was accidentally triggered when

I was with Heidi. Most people would panic. Heidi handled me with kindness, courage, and compassion, related qualities which are her trademark.

Heidi came right up to me and said,

"Calm down, Peter, it's OK."

I gradually pulled out of my rage and hugged Heidi and thanked her. Once again, Heidi saved many lives, including mine.

Heidi, The Prizefighter

Heidi had a long and distinguished prizefighting career. While my career was cut short by illness, injuries, and medication, she was still going strong at 43, well after most people had to stop. She was a natural fighter and I could tell she was good because she punched in combinations and on balance. Also, her solo punches had considerable authority.

She beat most of the women in tournaments, but found women too easy, so she preferred to fight men. She beat most of them, too, even with the handicap of a smashed leg. One time when fighting a big guy, he hit her hard and stunned her so she saw stars. But she had a will to win. She eluded him, recovered and overwhelmed him with a savage two-handed attack.

Heroine Heidi, The Social Worker

Heidi worked hard to get educated as a social worker. She was fantastic. She not only did her job faithfully as an outreach worker helping homeless and disadvantaged youth, but went above and beyond the call of duty. She spared no effort to get the children off the street and away from drugs. Sometimes, as a last resort she would give the children her own money so they would not resort to foul means to get it.

One time, someone started shooting up a school and firing on students. Heidi fearlessly rushed in and used her Tae Kwon Do to subdue, again saving many lives at great personal risk. She was eventually awarded a medal.

Heroine Heidi, The Woman

Although Heidi has many virtues, the measure of a woman is her ability to make a man feel like a man. Similarly the measure of a man is his ability to make a woman feel like a woman. There are some exceptions, though. Anyway, Heidi, with her vision and femininity does this well and is very emotionally satisfying.

Heidi's Life With Her Adoptive Family

Heidi was adopted by a warm, loving middle class family. It was much better than before. She was a good student, a loving daughter, and excelled at many sports. She has a muscular body and could probably have generated good running speed. Her favorite sports were Tae Kwon Do and boxing, both of which won her many medals. It takes a lot of courage to get into the ring with a partner, which she has. Heidi credits her great courage to participation in sports. Heidi also has a reluctance to hurt someone, which may have taken something away from her tremendous athletic ability, but she still achieved excellence. Her primary school days were relatively happy times as she went from student to athlete to home helper.

Things went along smoothly until at age 11 she began to blossom into a woman. She felt self-conscious about this at first. At age 11 she ran away from home, living by her wits, stealing, and living in hotels. She saw a very shady side of life, but still kept up a high moral standard of her own, albeit different, but principled nevertheless. Heidi managed to elude predators and bad people until police detectives found her and took her back to her good parents.

Things went well after that until she got pregnant at age 15, and the baby was given to her aunt to raise. Heidi was so upset that she ran away again and became homeless again. This time she supported herself with her feminine charms and made over a million dollars that she unselfishly gave to people she thought needed it. She was again found and brought back.

Her sexuality was beginning to show and she is more flexible and liberal than most people. She is attracted to both men and women, which is very rare. In all probability, she is predominantly attracted to men, but only she knows for sure. She treats people the best she can, but sometimes her temper gets in the way of that.

She has had many friends of both sexes and is an excellent catch, especially for a man. I would have snatched her up in an instant if I had not been married. She has had difficult relationships, perhaps because she needs love and looks for it in all the wrong places. Heidi has some very staunch friends who help her out, but her father is especially dedicated. He saved her life several times when she had problems such as an asthma attack and so on. He is a hero. Part of Heidi's problem in relationships could be that she does not recognize when she is loved and therefore is not receptive to it. She may reject people because of this.

I angered her greatly by calling too often and hanging up when she was telling me off for this. I also did some other things that were probably hurtful.

Heidi got pregnant by her staunch friend and it was a tubal pregnancy that is always dangerous. So great is her regard for life that she almost died because she would not terminate the pregnancy. Heidi also survived ovarian cancer with typical courage and aplomb. She is a true Superwoman.

At what was probably age 20, Heidi got married and had a fine daughter. Eight years later she got divorced, but is still friends with her ex-husband and helps her daughter. She also appreciates her ex-husband's dedication.

Heidi has an excellent resume and an excellent work resume in addition to her sports therapy. She is not the least bit lazy. A number of things to do with her counselling and life experiences led her into a sports therapy and problem-solving therapy practice. Anything could come through her door, or to cruelly harm her, but Heidi does not flinch.

Heidi's Therapy

Heidi takes a leadership role in her therapy practice driven by a powerful desire to help people and her caring attitude. She makes sure that clients are treated properly and the staff is treated properly. She often treats who want to be punished to rid guilt, which is where I fit in. I suspect that Heidi may have some of these tendencies herself, which is why she has so much feeling for us. She develops a rapport with all her clients and is one of the best of the many therapists and doctors I have seen.

The therapy practice is potentially dangerous because who knows what crazy people will use her service. I was a nuissance, but some people are stalkers and some can be cruel, and some people do not properly appreciate her, probably due to ignorance.

She gives enemas, boxing therapy, and many other types of therapy.

She told me she'd beat the crap out of me. In truth, she beat the sperm out of me, with her beauty, her kindness, and the right strength of punches and kicks. I have wanted to be beaten up since I was 10 and beaten up by a woman since age 13. My wife also packs a fabulous wallop. I hate hitting people and hitting a woman is out of the question.

Heidi may have been angry because I would not make love to her, but I dearly do not want to hurt my wife and the Jewish religion takes adultery very seriously.

As part of her practice, Heidi throws parties for friends and interested people. Heidi is a leader. The Argos had a star player, Terry Metcalf whom they called "The Franchise" and "Sweetfeet" for his dazzling running style. I sometimes call Heidi "Sweetfists" for her dazzling boxing skills.

Heidi is so beautiful and exciting that I often think about her along with my wife, sometimes to completion. I love Heidi along with my wife and I want you to love her too, and pray for her.

Heidi-Finding True Love

In order to find someone who will love Heidi and appreciate her the way I do, she must first stay around people she wants to meet. This would be in church groups, in athletic clubs, by introduction from good friends, by good dating services, by ads on Kijiji, newspaper ads, cultural clubs ad infinitum. Meeting someone through her work or something like that would lead to the wrong people, like Jeff. She already has a great father and another staunch friend besides myself.

Heidi is brave and bold and that will help her meet people. She must meet someone sincere and make sure he respects her. She should avoid sex at first until she gets to know him well. They should exchange ideas, opinions, interests, and must talk about themselves and get to know each other. Again, Heidi's candidness would help here. They must respect each other as people, men and women.

They should go on dates to art galleries, museums, movies, meals, science centres, meet together and so on. She must wait for Mr. Right and have the right kind of fussiness, a mix of acknowledging love and respect, and waiting for it. She is worth it.

My Dream – Treating Heidi Like The Queen and Angel She Is

Don Quixote, the Man of La Mancha had a quest:

To dream the impossible dream; To fight the unbeatable foe;

To bear with unbearable sorrow; To run where the brave dare not go; To right the unrightable wrong; To love pure and chaste from afar; To try when your arms are too weary;

To reach the unreachable star; This is my quest; To follow that star; No matter how hopeless; No matter how far; To fight for the right; without question or pause; To be willing to march into hell for a heavenly cause; And I know if I'll only be true in this glorious quest; That my heart will lie peaceful and calm when I'm laid to my rest; And the world will be better for this; That one man scorned and covered with scars; Still strove with his last ounce of courage; To reach the unreachable star.

This is the romantic side of me. I am not close to perfect, great, or even good. We must accept ourselves for who we are and accept our loved ones for both the good and the bad. We can then accentuate the good and downplay the bad.

Heidi, by inspiring me brings out the best in me. It is a romantic style called quixotic, after Don Quixote. She even makes me a better husband to my wife.

Love is defined as a will to extend yourself to promote the spiritual growth, mental health and well-being of someone. Hatred is defined as a will to stifle yourself to promote the spiritual hurting of someone. As part of our love we must strive to become the best we can be and help others be the best they can be. Because Heidi does this for so many, she is greatness personified, a true love goddess.

I wish someone (I'd love to) could provide her with a good home, good food, companionship, love, and let her be what she wants and have what he is able to provide. It is OK for me to provide this as a friend, but I cannot be the one and only she needs obviously.

We must and can help each other spiritually, physically, intellectually, socially, emotionally, and financially. I love Heidi and expect nothing in return. I grow from this.

Another chapter in Heidi's life shows her heart of gold. I did not fully realize the full extent of her depth of character and sensitivity to other peoples' suffering and other peoples' words. She originally showed this when she told me it was about time I forgave myself for something I did 46 years ago.

Heidi developed a relationship with a cancer patient and stuck with him through thick and thin. He abused her terribly, swore at her, punched her, kicked her, especially in her sore leg, called her horrible, inaccurate names, made her wait on him, ruined her health, stalked her, would not give her money or let her eat and so on ad nauseam. Heidi was so sensitive that when she was going to leave him and he would cry like a baby, she would go back to him.

Eventually, I got so outraged that I went to his house to bolster her extraction. He denied that she was there and went back and abused her. Heidi bravely left him. Her father eventually put her up and I felt relieved. I thought it would be hard to handle two beauty queens at once.

Heidi is a true angel, who enriches all the lives she touches. I went to her for help and she gave it to me as she does to all. I thought of asking her father, a minister for help.

Finally, Heidi settled in to our home and my wife accepts her and I feel OK again.

Heidi vs The Mass Murderer

Heidi has had a fascinating life story. Here is another part to it. When Heidi lived in Parkdale, she befriended a man who was very charming. He pretended to do good things for Heidi and many other women. In truth, he was the devil's son. A number of ladies of the night were disappearing and Heidi happened to catch on to him. She mentioned it to him and he said no. When he got her up in his apartment, he locked the door and came in lunging at her with two butcher knives. The only escape was to jump out the window. She landed four floors below and suffered a compound fracture to her right fibula, splitting the right lateral malleolus. She needed surgery and several skin grafts, eventually. It never healed properly and doctors thought she would never walk again. She escaped to police and told them what had happened and they looked for the man. He ran away to the United States and was never caught.

Meanwhile, Heidi defied the odds and learned to both walk and run. Awesome!

Heidi vs Killer Clients

One time Heidi agreed to go up to two male clients' home and be tied up. She was also naked. However, it soon became clear that they intended to attack her and kill her, which would have been easy, since she was bound tightly. Heidi used her strength and self-defense techniques to get rid of the restraints, get her clothes and run, leaving the two creepy men frustrated and wondering what had happened. Another chapter in the adventures of Superwoman!

E-Mails with Heidi and Ms. Nadja, Dominatrices

It can be seen from the emails, the tremendous esteem that dominatrices and their clients usually hold each other in and usually have corresponding paraphilias. Heidi was a warmer personality. The other dominatrix was more professional and aloof, but sympathetic. I felt love feelings toward both of them. Both women punched hard and gave good beatings, but Heidi put more decorations on my face and body, perhaps due to her karate background.

E-Mails with Heidi

March 28, 2015

Peter Cohen wrote:

Dear Heidi,

I'm so glad I met you. You are an outstanding person and woman. I will probably have some time Tues. to help ghost write your book. I will try to call you when I can. Also, that was a nice beating you gave me.

Thank you, love, Pete

Heidi wrote:

Your turning me on. I understand. Your making my clit ring tingle. Your a class act. I love the fact that you love to be beaten. I also went through a time when I had to be choked as well as fucked in the ass.

PC wrote: To my beautiful, brainy, and brave friend, Heidi,

I know you have had a lot of pain in life. I want to do what I can to make it better. Please think of ways I can help. Also, thank you for your wonderful therapy. I feel a lot better now. I might be thinking of you a lot because I have obsessive tendencies. Also, you showed great mercy because you probably could have snapped me like a matchstick. I hope you realize how great you are.

Love, Pete

PC – Heidi, please do not allow anyone to hurt you.

HG – Thank God I was thinking about you, today.

HG – I love my father. I don't know what to do. I'm so used to having him around.

HG – Good job my father loves me doesn't he????

HG – They say life is what you make it.

PC – Re: Preciousness – To my beautiful, brainy, and brave friend, Heidi. Thank you so much for the benefits from your wonderful beating. I will be grateful forever. It was courageous, gallant, and unselfish on your part. It takes a lot of courage to train for boxing. I would like to meet you tomorrow 9am Tuesday to discuss your autobiography. I would not commit adultery because I would feel terrible if I did. I know you understand.

Love and admiration, Pete

PC – I found your story very sad and depressing. Let me know if you want me to continue with it. Hope you are well and whatever happened was my fault.

Yours, Peter

PC – I managed to download some of your pictures finally. You are extremely beautiful. I have been appointed president of AA as the biggest asshole in the world.

- Peter

PC – Re: great healer

Dear Heidi,

Even the doctor was delighted in my improvement from your beating. It relieved my conscience. Bless you forever. You should legitimately be called doctor. I wish you only good things. You are very humanitarian.

Your friend, Pete

PC – Dear Heidi,

I hope you are not so angry with me that you will not give me one of your fabulous beatings. We men only respond to physical correction.

Thank you, Peter

HG – Re great healer – Thanks. I'm very stresses out about money and stuff that's all. Thanks for your kind words.

PC – Let me know if there is something I can do to help within reason.

HG – Thank you. I'm waiting for my income tax money. I filed for 6 years. I'm going to receive over 4000 and over 2900 in GST and Trillium. I've managed to pay everyone back thus far with my advertising as a sex therapist. However, I could not afford to make the newspaper as just online this week. As I told you I've been looking for one pornography film then this will be behind me no one knows how much of a struggle its been on me. Even buy a book for class – So yes My gratefulness will be never-ending if you could help me with my problem, mr moneybags mmmm I will be your private boxer for as long as its okay with you. I'm very excited about beating your ass. I know how it hurts you as well as beating your face over and over and over again the way you deserve to be beaten because you are a very very uncooperative disobedient selfish man who needs a lot of healing.

PC – Dear Heidi, Thank you for your kind offer, but if you read my book, It Takes A Woman, you will find that I have been down that path and it had a bad outcome for all parties.

Yours, Pete

PC – Dear Heidi, You have beauty, perseverance, courage and compassion. Someone like that will always succeed at whatever she wants to be.

Love, Pete

PC – Dear Heidi, I can't thank you enough for the wonderful beating you gave me. I am very grateful.

Love, Pete

HG – Your welcome.

PC – A glorious death – Dear Heidi, I feel a calm, peaceful serenity as I feel that death is imminent. You can be proud that you are one of the few people that never hurt me. Mental pain is much worse than physical pain. You are very beautiful inside and out and I regret that I have nothing to leave behind. I want to lie down and die. Love to you and all good people forever. Thank you for your help and pain relief.

Your friend, Pete

HG – Peter you can't give up.

HG – Right now I have no money at all and I thought of taking my own life as well.

HG – Peter, I just spoke to your wife. I was afraid when I read your email. Pls call me.

HG – Call me pater

PC – I have no thought of taking my life. I only feel that I do not have much longer to live and am happy. I talked to Scott of Now magazine who said an ad would cost 61 dollars. I do not know if that would be a good idea. Give me a call.

PC – My shortcomings – I am very stupid, a slow learner, and a mean, rotten guy. At least you are good as are many others.

Sincerely, Pete

PC – Cruisin' for a bruisin'

Dear Heidi I might need help with another beating. I am very bad and mean and only respond to physical correction.

Love, Pete

PC – Get well soon – Dear Heidi,

I hope you recover soon and completely. That is the main thing. You might as well ignore the perverted stuff I sent you.

Yours, Pete

HG – I've been reading your book. Well done, Mr. C. I'm impressed.

PC – You are a beautiful person and also have two of the most beautiful... fists that you use courageously.

HG – Thank you. I miss you. xoxoxoxo

PC – I hope you are doing well. Congratulations on cutting down to two cigarrettes a day. I will tell you when I am over my infection.

PC – I'm a very mean, vile, despicable man and will only respond to physical correction.

HG – I loved you.

PC – I love you, too, Heidi. The sweetest pair of fists in Toronto have probably done a lot of people much good.

Yours, Pete

PC – Remorse

Dear Heidi,

I am very sorry that I mistreated you and caused a bad feeling. Would beating the crap out of me help you to feel better? I will accept any punishment you offer short of anything immoral. My conscience is hurting. You are worth your weight in gold, your brains are superior and your fists are like gold.

I love you, Pete

HG – Actually peter it would. I'm really in the mood to beat the shit out of you badly.

PC – Thank you. When can we arrange a time and place. It will make us both feel better.

Love, Pete

PC – It takes a great deal of courage for a woman to hit a man, especially therapeutically. Even if the man does not hit, it is like a surgeon cutting into flesh and healing. You would have made a great doctor. I am excited about seeing you.

Love, Pete

PC – Dear Heidi,

You are great.

Love, Pete

HG – I am, so is my clit ring. Do you wanna get married?

PC - Yes, very much so. But it would be illegal and immoral as I am already married.

PC – You're the greatest. You're the prettiest and middleweight champion of Toronto since you defeated me.

Love, Pete

HG – I need pills. Please call.

PC – I'm reluctant to call you for fear of disturbing you so I don't.

Yours, Pete

HG – Don't be. Sometimes you call and I don't get there and I feel sad, very very sad.

PC – Happy mother's day.

HG – Thank you, Peter. I love what you've written so far. Pls. Bring some clonazepam as many as possible without bringing harm to yourself and chocolate. It would mean the work to me baby.

I love you very much. Your wife's a very lucky lady. I'm afraid I do envy her. That's why I was so mean the other day. I'm sorry. I'm going to bed now my ringer's off. Would like to see you around one. That would be awesome.

PC – OK, champ. Hope you feel better.

PC – I love you my sweet archangel.

HG – I love the book thus far. Dr. Ghost's such a hot name. Hmmm.

PC – Re: honesty

Dear Heidi,

You have to take with a grain with a grain of salt what people say when they are emotional or sexually aroused. Love is not sex and sex is not love. Love is a will to extend yourself to promote the spiritual growth of someone. We had that, it is a question of acknowledging it.

Peter

After I hung up on a verbal spanking the following email resulted.

HG – Re: I don't like your rude tone so go fuck yourself with the highest regards PETER. If that doesn't work your wife can suffocate you; You little pompous piece of NOTHINGNESS. I would tell you to go to hell but I know you're already there so if you value your nose and teeth stay clear right now. PETER you are lower than shit the dog ate and vommitted again LOLOLOLOLOL. IDIOT. FOOL I now find distasteful.

PC – Thank you and bless you.

PC – Heidi, I don't blame you for anything. Whatever happened was my fault. You gave me what I deserved.

Thank you, Pete

PC – I have always longed to be punched, kicked, sworn at and degraded by a beautiful woman. I would like to be beaten to death by you but sadly that will not happen because you are too angry to oblige me. You have the finest fists and feet in the world but hopefully someone will do the honours.

Love, Pete

HG – Till we apologize you can call me.

PC – Heidi, I'm very sorry about what I did to you. I hung up on you, missed appointments, called too often and did not always call when I missed appointments. My behaviour was childish, heartless, and reprehensible and obviously hurt a good and sensitive woman. Also, I think I sent two sarcastic and disparaging emails I did not mean. Please feel free to call anytime and say what I did. Also, I should not use three dangerous words.

Sincerely, Peter

HG – Hi baby I'm sorry.

PC – I'm sorry, too. Sometimes we lose sight of our objectives. Also we seem to have extremes of love and hate which is not good.

Peter

PC – you win.

Dear Heidi,

You win. You're the all time champion. You can knock me out with your beauty, your athletic skills, or your personality, you win. You're a beautiful, busty, black goddess. You're hot. I'm not. You excite me no end. If you're going to beat me up, please do it with love. Thank you for some great times and I'm sorry I hurt you.

Love and best wishes, Peter

PC – Heidi, You ARE a great writer. I have never seen such powerful and descriptive language as what you used. You're going to do a great job writing a book that only you can write.

Love, Pete

PC – Heidi, please hit me. Beat me to death. I love you and deserve it.

HG – Your rude. Sometimes I will.

PC – Heidi, do you want me to finish your book.

HG – Of course, u little bitch. How else would I get to punch you in the face.

PC – To rid the world of a creep like me would be courageous, gallant, and unselfish. My last words would be I love you.

PC – Re: A human heavy bag and your fan.

Hit me like the heavy bag. Hit me like the heavy bag. You're the greatest. You're the prettiest. The people's champion. I should get down on my hands and knees and kiss you feet, then kiss up your body to your fabulous fists, the finest fists in the world. They heal. Everyone loves you. I love your punches. You hit as hard as a 300 pound woman.

Your adoring and grateful fan, Peter

PC – One to beat up, champ. I hope you break my jaw.

PC – Longing to taste your sweet knuckle sandwiches. I'm sorry about what I did.

PC – Re: depression

Dear Heidi,

How are you? I'm feeling low now and a good beating would be nice. However, I think I'm in the doghouse.

Your friend (I hope), Pete

HG – We will have to get together ASAP. I have been homeless for 3 weeks. I've even had to sleep in my dads minivan for 2 out of 3 weeks and live in hotels when friends and family have the money.

PC – Heidi, This is terrible. Come to my house. You are of fine character.

PC – very bad

Heidi, I have been very bad and no punishment is too severe. This is a job for Superwoman. You can give me just punishment and I am extremely sorry.

A despicable creep named Peter

PC – work

It's just a job. Waves wash over the sands. Birds fly in the sky. The sun rises in the morning. The moon rises at night. You beat people up. - adapted from Muhammad Ali.

You do it with love and compassion.

PC – don't hurt yourself. That is my main plea.

HG – I love having my nipples pinched when I masturbate now that my clit is pierced I can cum very easily. It's amazing. I know if I pierce my nipples I can cum from the pain. I can feel my father's energy. He's probably outside my home. I started drinking again because I felt guilty about turning my father on. I feel terrible my father is into me the way he is. I was angry at my mother. She told me a big lie about my daughter being given up for adoption. After 8 or so months had passed, I felt this emptiness that I can't even explain. The first few nights after the adoption I missed her. I didn't know what to do so I left home and went down to Lakeshore and hooked until I had enough money for a hotel room for a few nights and a large bottle of Bacardi. I saw a guy I knew from when I would hook to get money when I was pregnant.

HG – Peter, I think your amazing. You are a good man. I love you. Thank you my friend. I will let you come tomorrow at 12. I miss you. I'll take my chances because your my friend and I love you. Xoxoxo

HG- sorry if I hurt you and nahla. I love you both very much.

HG – I guess I'm a bully. What can I say.

PC – No, Heidi, you are the farthest thing from a bully. You are brave, mature, and honest and gave me what I deserved. You are a wonderful and beautiful woman and I'm glad I met you.

HG – Peter, I have a short story they wrote about me while I was at the treatment centre. I hated it. I cried everyday for a month. I'll be honest with you. I do love you; I also admire you your a good man. That wife of yours does not know how blessed she is to have you. Wouldn't that be funny if she was actually cheating on you.

E-Mails with Ms Nadja von Sade

Most of these emails come from me, but two of them come from her. There are about 38 in total. Again, you can see the tremendous esteem I hold her in. This time, the high regard is more on my part.

PC – Dear Ms Nadja,

Thank you so much for agreeing to beat me up as therapy for my guilt. I have never hit a woman and it is out of the question. I have injured arms as well and cannot hit anything. I have some injuries because I used to be an amateur boxer and can take a lot of punishment. Taking punishment is the only skill I retain from boxing. I intensely dislike hitting people outside the ring and have this problem because I once hit a man outside the ring. My masochism gets bad when my mental disorder flares up. I am on medication for it but sometimes my guilt gets bad. Many people feel I deserve the death penalty. You are being very compassionate by giving me this treatment and sparing my life. It is very heroic. When a woman hits me, I get very excited and affectionate and tend to fall in love. This happened with a lady dominatrix who was a professional boxer and karate expert. She stayed at my place when she became homeless but I had to kick her out when she was rude to my wife and I. My wife is very strong and is kind enough to hit me at times, but I feel I would like some professional assistance.

Forever grateful, Peter

Ms Nadja – Hello, Peter. I appreciate the thoughtfulness of your letter and look forward to punishing you tomorrow.

PC – Dear Ms Nadja, (fondness) Thank you so much for the wonderful work you did with me. It made me feel much better. I'm sorry I ended the session early but you were much better than I thought. You punched hard and it was a good experience. If I need another treatment I will definitely come back to you. You also have a delightful personality and were very professional. You are beautiful, inside and out.

With gratitude and fondness, Peter

PC – Tremendous fondness and gratitude

Dear Ms Nadja, I noticed that the anger, guilt, and depression that characterize my illness are greatly improved. People do sports for the same reason people become physicians. You helped me immensely, similar to the best doctors in the world.

Thine eternally, Peter

PC – justice – Dear Ms Nadja,

You are a true Superwoman, meting out justice in such a courageous, gallant, and unselfish way. You gave me exactly what I deserved, similar to what I did to my victim. I feel much better after your treatment. You may even have eased up my masochism. Your boyfriend or husband must love you very much. You also helped my relationship with my wife. Forgive me for feeling love, but you were very professional and did not force me to love you. I notice that you have an excellent command of English and know at least one other language. I think you are of high intelligence and are a woman of many parts. You have many skills and talents. Your inner beauty accentuates your outer beauty.

Sincerely, Peter

Ms Nadja felt that my emails were sincere.

PC – powers – Dear Ms Nadja,

I am fantasizing that if I need help, I can call out to you for help and you will come to my rescue. I am forever in your debt. Since I was not sexually excited, it hurt and was true justice.

PC – goodness – You have the sweetest pair of fists and feet in the business. Thank you for being you.

PC – healing and gratefulness – I can't thank you enough for the fantastic treatment you gave me. It was a good beating and you may be the fastest and hardest hitting person who has ever hit me. You are my Joan of Arc and my Superwoman. You taught me a good lesson.

PC – Your treatments are a growth experience for anyone who wants them. I feel much better and am a better person.

PC – You my beautiful, brainy and brave friend will always keep me on the right path with your sweet fists and feet.

PC – Courageous is someone you like and cowardly is someone you do not like and I like you so much. You use your hands like a great surgeon. You use seemingly harsh techniques to heal people. You are one of the kindest, nicest, most beautiful, caring, mature and together persons I have met. May you enjoy peace, health, happiness and prosperity forever. I feel like I may finally be free after 48 years of problem.

PC – You're all woman. And one of the finest women I have ever met, next to my wife. You are very exciting and emotionally satisfying.

PC – Dear Ms Nadja (nobility) Thank you for your noble attempts to help me. To hug a monster like me twice took enormous courage and makes me very fond of you. Even though you are great, my serious brain disease is not in your field. We all try our best. Hopefully, I will be somewhat different after your kind and noble treatment of me. - Live long and prosper from Peter

PC – The good fight – I long for the feel of your fabulous, feminine fists against my face and body. You fought my demons and I so bravely. All the while I could have turned into a 7 foot, 500 pound green skinned monster. I feel a lot better after some antipsychotic medication and meeting such a brave, beautiful, bodacious woman like you was a growth experience.

PC – You gave me a great Christmas present – a much needed pair of socks from your two fists. It took great courage for you to do this as you risked my coming back and hitting you. You said you would punish me to get rid of my guilt. You kept your word. I hope you enjoyed giving the treatment because I enjoyed getting it. You saved my life very heroically sparing me from the death penalty.

Love, Pete

PC – A good experience – You have one of the most beautiful minds I have ever seen. I have never seen anyone with your depth of understanding before. When you stood in front of me, brazenly showing your completely naked fists and letting me enjoy their sight, I knew you would do a first class job. Your fists were so sexy and exciting and your feet were beautiful. Your face and figure were mesmerizing. You delighted me with punches I could only hear and not see. Your brain is very precious and does great thinking to help people. I feel I could tell you anything. You obviously attend to everything people say.

It was only the second time I had ever been slugged by a full grown woman's completely naked fists. It was delightful and exciting. You were kind and gentle and I did not hurt at all. Using your sensuous fists on my near virgin face, you must be a goddess. I feel I can do whatever I want and you will therapy me.

Loving you, Peter

PC – Goddess stature – You were so beautiful standing there, your naked fists magnificent over your strong, powerful arms. All woman. I took a lot of grit to develop your body and athletic skills. It takes a lot of courage to apply these skills to help someone like me.

Love you from Peter

PC – Nobody has treated me as you have. But for Superwoman it's all in a day's work. You were also merciful, kind, and professional with my love.

PC – angel – You're an angel. Your punches came straight from heaven which is why I could not see them. You saved me from Satan's power. Guilt and anger are twin ills of the amygdala of the limbic system governing emotion in the brain, overreactive with schizophrenia. With good therapy and good medical management we can beat this. I am very fortunate.

Bless you, Peter

PC – Dear Ms Nadja, I have great news. I'm going into remission. I even stopped begging my wife to hit me. I hope you are doing well as you deserve the best.

Ms Nadja – I am happy you are in a better place, mentally. It would be My pleasure to see you for treatment should you wish to return. - Stay healthy from Ms Nadja von Sade

PC – sexiness and beauty

Your fists are the most beautiful and exciting I have ever seen. They are big, sensuous and full. They complement your excellent figure and athletic skills nicely. You use them to mete out justice in such a courageous, gallant, and unselfish way. The thought of your wonderful beatings gets me very excited.

Love, Petev

9 781726 293846